Original title:
After the Fall

Copyright © 2024 Swan Charm
All rights reserved.

Author: Aron Pilviste
ISBN HARDBACK: 978-9916-79-105-9
ISBN PAPERBACK: 978-9916-79-106-6
ISBN EBOOK: 978-9916-79-107-3

A Canvas of Forgotten Stories

Beneath the faded sky, dreams soar high,
Brush strokes of time, where shadows lie.
Whispers of laughter hang in the air,
Echoes of voices, stories laid bare.

Colors of memory, a palette of glum,
Faded photographs, where we all come from.
Silent reflections in the evening light,
A canvas of tales lost in the night.

Voices Beneath the Ruins

Amidst crumbling stones, the past unfolds,
Ancient whispers of secrets untold.
Echoes of joy wrapped in sorrow's veil,
Lives once vibrant, now a ghostly trail.

In the shadows, memories intertwine,
The laughter of children, faint yet divine.
Roots of time clutch deep in the ground,
Voices of history, forever profound.

Whispers of the Broken Leaves

Gentle breezes carry tales of the old,
Leaves rustle softly, their stories unfold.
Each crackle and crunch holds a piece of the past,
Whispers of nature, in silence amassed.

Fragile and fleeting, the seasons do change,
Yet the essence of life feels oddly strange.
In the dance of decay, beauty survives,
Whispers of the broken, where hope still thrives.

Voices Beneath the Ruins

Amidst crumbling stones, the past unfolds,
Ancient whispers of secrets untold.
Echoes of joy wrapped in sorrow's veil,
Lives once vibrant, now a ghostly trail.

In the shadows, memories intertwine,
The laughter of children, faint yet divine.
Roots of time clutch deep in the ground,
Voices of history, forever profound.

Whispers of the Broken Leaves

Gentle breezes carry tales of the old,
Leaves rustle softly, their stories unfold.
Each crackle and crunch holds a piece of the past,
Whispers of nature, in silence amassed.

Fragile and fleeting, the seasons do change,
Yet the essence of life feels oddly strange.
In the dance of decay, beauty survives,
Whispers of the broken, where hope still thrives.

Echoes of a Swaying Silence

In the stillness of night, shadows confess,
A symphony sweet in the quietness.
Each sigh of the wind tells a tale so grand,
Echoes of silence, a soft, gentle hand.

Beneath the moon's gaze, dreams drift away,
In the heart of the dark, night beats like clay.
A hush in the air, holding each breath tight,
Echoes of a sway, lost in the night.

Threads of Vanished Light

In twilight's soft embrace we find,
Whispers of a day that's passed us by.
Golden strands of dreams unwind,
Beneath the fading, endless sky.

Ghosts of laughter fill the air,
Dancing shadows, lost in time.
A tapestry of moments rare,
Sewn with memories, pure and prime.

Flickers of hope, they shimmer bright,
Guiding us through the obscured night.
Each stitch a story, bold and slight,
Tangled paths in their gentle flight.

Yet as the stars begin to glow,
These threads will fade, they will not stay.
They beckon softly, like rivers flow,
Carrying our hearts, so far away.

In silence we gather, hand in hand,
Holding tight to the light we knew.
With every strand we make our stand,
Threads of vanished light, forever true.

The Last Sigh of Autumn

Leaves that dance in shades of gold,
Whisper tales in the crisp, cool air.
Stories of warmth, now growing cold,
As the season sheds its vibrant flair.

Beneath the boughs, soft breezes sigh,
A lullaby for the fading light.
Nature weeps as the branches cry,
For the fleeting days turning to night.

Crisp air cloaks the fading hue,
Colors drain like whispers lost.
Retention falters, a memory's due,
In the quiet, we count the cost.

Frost-kissed mornings awaken slow,
Glimmers of winter approach with grace.
Autumn bows with a final glow,
Leaving shadows where sunshine plays.

As we linger, we'll hold it close,
The last sigh of a world so bright.
In our hearts, it gently grows,
Memories cherished, lost from sight.

Unraveling the Echoes

In the halls where silence lingers,
Footsteps trace forgotten dreams.
Each whisper pulls on faded fingers,
Treading the path of fractured seams.

Shadows dance where light once played,
Murmurs of lives that once did thrive.
Fragments of laughter, joy now frayed,
In the echoes, we fight to survive.

A voice calls out, a distant chime,
Through tangled thoughts of yesterday.
The heart can beat, can bend with time,
Yet still it yearns for the lost array.

Threads of memory, they weave and wane,
Drawing us back to places dear.
In every note, a hint of pain,
But in the melody, hope draws near.

As night unfolds its quiet shroud,
We gather the echoes, piece by piece.
In the silence, we stand unbowed,
Holding tight to the heart's sweet release.

Driftwood on a Forgotten Shore

Washed by tides of time and fate,
Driftwood rests upon the sand.
Carved by storms, it contemplates,
A life once led, a journey planned.

Each knot and swirl, a story told,
Of wanderings 'neath vast, blue skies.
With salt-stained memories, bold and old,
It listens to the ocean's sighs.

The sun dips low, a fiery glow,
Painting shadows on the weary wood.
In ebb and flow, the silence grows,
A testament of all that stood.

As night unfolds its starry quilt,
The driftwood whispers to the waves.
In quiet moments, dreams are built,
Upon the past that time engraves.

So let it rest on that lonely shore,
A piece of time, both calm and deep.
In every grain, the ocean's lore,
Driftwood holds the secrets we keep.

Shadows of Yesterday

In twilight's glow, we wander slow,
Whispers of dreams, in ebb and flow.
Memories linger, soft as a sigh,
Haunting the spaces where echoes lie.

Faded images, etched in time,
Dancing like leaves, in rhythm and rhyme.
The heart recalls what the mind conceals,
A tapestry woven with what it feels.

Each shadow tells of love and loss,
Carved in the night, we bear the cross.
In every corner where light may stray,
We find ourselves in shadows of yesterday.

The Silence that Remains

In stillness deep, where whispers wane,
Echoes fade like a distant train.
Words unspoken, heavy with hue,
Paint the silence in shades of blue.

A pause can speak what voices cannot,
Murmurs of truths in the quiet plot.
Hearts intertwined, yet worlds apart,
Finding solace in the silent art.

Every heartbeat a delicate thrum,
In the hush of night, we become numb.
Beneath the weight of what's not said,
Lingers the silence that softly led.

Fragments of a Distant Bloom

In gardens lost, where colors fade,
Petals whisper of dreams betrayed.
Time's gentle hand, it shifts the light,
Leaving traces of old delight.

Each fragment speaks of sun and rain,
Gathering stories, mingled with pain.
Blooming once bright, now quiet and still,
Awaiting the moments that time will distill.

In memories held like treasures rare,
Fleeting glances of what was there.
A distant scent on the evening air,
Still lingers softly in the heart's care.

Stones Beneath the Surface

Beneath the waves where shadows play,
Lie secrets hidden, far away.
Smooth stones glimmer in twilight's dance,
Guarding stories of chance and romance.

Each ripple tells of the paths we've crossed,
Yet in the depths, so much is lost.
The surface sparkles, a false display,
For what lies below, it seldom sways.

In quiet waters, where silence dwells,
Echoes linger, the heart compels.
To seek the truth in the cool embrace,
Of stones beneath the surface's grace.

The Season of Unraveled Hopes

Leaves fall gently from trees,
Whispers of dreams caught in air.
Promises dance on the breeze,
Unraveled hopes linger there.

Morning dew clings to the ground,
Echoes of laughter start to fade.
In silence, we search all around,
For lost moments, unmade.

The sunlight dims as time goes on,
Shadows stretch on the weary track.
Though some days feel hopelessly gone,
We gather strength to push back.

Each turn brings a new surprise,
Blossoms sprout from cracked stone.
Letting go, we start to rise,
In the garden of the alone.

Roots entwine beneath the dust,
Channeling strength from the past.
In winter, we find our trust,
New seasons of hope are cast.

Clarity in the Dusk of Despair

Shadows dance under fading light,
Fractured dreams linger near.
In the silence of the night,
Hope glimmers, though unclear.

As stars emerge in the gloom,
Lessons learned from the fight.
Through silence blooms a new bloom,
A soft breath, a spark of light.

Voices whisper from the heart,
Calling softly through the dark.
In the stillness, we will start,
To uncover each hidden spark.

With each tear and heavy sigh,
Strength is found and we rise.
Through the veil, we learn to fly,
Finding truths beneath the lies.

In the dusk, clarity's grace,
Painting shadows with intent.
In despair, we find our place,
A journey of dreams well spent.

Uncharted Paths of Rebirth

New dawn breaks with gentle light,
Paths unfurl that once were tight.
Every step a leap of faith,
Unseen roads begin to wraith.

The sky is painted in gold hues,
Each color whispers a chance.
Life invites us to choose,
In its rhythm, we shall dance.

With the wind tracing our way,
We embrace what lies ahead.
Each moment is a chance to play,
As past sorrows gently shed.

Mountains loom and valleys call,
Echoes of dreams in the deep.
Together, we will not fall,
In this journey, our tales sweep.

Trust in the steps we will take,
With every fall, we rise anew.
Uncharted paths, the dawn will make,
With hearts strong, we'll carry through.

The Ashes of Yesterday's Glory

In the embers lies a tale,
Of triumph and the weary fight.
What once glowed, now seems pale,
In shadows lost to fading light.

Echoes of laughter softly ring,
Memories wrapped in the night.
From ashes, we begin to sing,
Finding strength in our plight.

Through the pain, the lessons learned,
Life's flame flickers, then ignites.
As future's pages are turned,
Hope emerges from the heights.

With each breath, we rise anew,
Embracing the scars that remain.
In the heart lies a spirit true,
From ashes, we grow without chain.

Yesterday's glories softly fade,
Yet in the heart, they still reside.
With every step, new paths are laid,
A rebirth born from the tide.

Potions of the Past

In amber flasks, old whispers dwell,
Stories brewed, like secret spells.
Faded labels tell of grace,
Eras gone, in this small space.

Dusty shelves, where dreams reside,
Memories swirl, like a tide.
Elixirs sweet, each drop a sigh,
For lost moments, we still cry.

Charmed ingredients, roots of lore,
Each potion opens a hidden door.
Time's embrace in every sip,
Life reflected in every drip.

Crafted wonders, wisdom gained,
From potions made, our hearts unchained.
With every taste, we travel far,
To past's embrace, a guiding star.

In twilight's glow, the past awakes,
With every draught, a heart that aches.
Yet through the pain, the love returns,
In potions poured, our spirit yearns.

Reverie Amongst the Remains

In silent ruins where shadows play,
The echoes of lives long passed away.
Amidst the stones, a story breathes,
Of whispered dreams and tangled leaves.

Each broken wall, a tale to tell,
Of laughter, heartache, and hope that fell.
In quiet corners, the memories weave,
A tapestry of all that we grieve.

Time's gentle touch has carved the earth,
In every crevice, whispers of birth.
Where once were voices, now silence reigns,
Yet in that stillness, the spirit gains.

Amongst the shards, a beauty lies,
In what was lost, a glimpse of skies.
Reverie flows through the cracks of fate,
Where past and present intertwine and wait.

So linger long in this sacred space,
Embrace the echoes, the time, the grace.
For in the ruins, we find our thread,
A haunting melody of love not dead.

An Overture of New Beginnings

As dawn breaks forth, a canvas clear,
Brush strokes of light, hopes reappear.
With every hue, the shadows flee,
An overture of what can be.

Fresh blossoms bloom in tender light,
Promising days that feel so right.
Each petal whispers, 'life anew,'
In every heart, a dream breaks through.

The winds of change begin to blow,
Through open hearts, the warmth will flow.
With every step, a path unfolds,
A journey bright with stories told.

In laughter shared, in kindest deeds,
New beginnings grow like vibrant seeds.
So take a breath, embrace the chance,
In life's sweet dance, we all advance.

Together we rise, hand in hand,
In unity, we take our stand.
An overture, a song so grand,
A melody that rings throughout the land.

Beneath the Weight of Time

Beneath the weight of gentle hours,
Moments bloom like fragile flowers.
Each tick, a choice, each tock, a dream,
A river flows, a steady stream.

In twilight's glow, reflections cast,
The present holds the echoes past.
A tapestry woven, threads entwined,
In time's embrace, our stories find.

Lost in the maze where memories dwell,
Time whispers softly, like a spell.
Yet through the layers, bright sparks ignite,
Illuminating paths through the night.

With every heartbeat, we remain,
In shadows deep, in joyous rain.
Beneath the weight, we stand so tall,
In life's embrace, we feel it all.

So let us dance, let us be free,
In the arms of time, just you and me.
For underneath it all, we see the truth,
In every moment, lies our youth.

In the Guardian's Shadow

Beneath the towering oak's embrace,
Whispers of ages echo in grace.
Roots entangled, secrets unfurl,
Time's gentle hand, a tender whirl.

Sunlight dances on ancient bark,
Stories linger, leaving a mark.
Eyes closed, we breathe in the past,
Moments cherished, forever cast.

In the guardian's shadow we find,
The threads of memory intertwined.
A sanctuary where spirits roam,
In hearts of those who call it home.

The rustle of leaves, a soft sigh,
Echoes the dreams that never die.
Tales of love, loss, and rebirth,
In every corner, the weight of worth.

As twilight fades, the stars ignite,
Guiding our souls into the night.
In the silence, we discern the call,
In the guardian's shadow, we stand tall.

Fragments of a Dreamt Past

In the attic, dust and dreams collide,
Fragments of stories refuse to hide.
Cracked photographs whisper of light,
Captured moments, fading from sight.

Echoes of laughter, shadows of tears,
Woven together, the fabric of years.
Voices linger, soft as a breeze,
Remembering love, lost memories tease.

Time's gentle hands, a painter's brush,
Colors of sorrow, joy, and hush.
Each piece a puzzle we yearn to find,
Fragments of past, forever entwined.

In the silence, we piece it all,
Reconstructing the stories we'd recall.
Each thread a connection, fragile yet strong,
In fragments of a dreamt past, we belong.

The heart beats softly, a steady rhyme,
In the tapestry spun through the threads of time.
Gathering memories, sweet and bitter,
Fragments of a life that once felt bigger.

Gazing at the Ruins of Tomorrow

Upon the hill where shadows play,
Ruins whisper what words can't say.
Stone and dust, a testament stand,
Remnants of dreams, once grand.

Faded arches under fading skies,
Hold echoes of laughter, hopeful cries.
Moss-clad memories weave through the dark,
In the ruins of tomorrow, we leave our mark.

Time's gentle hand wears everything down,
Once golden crowns now turned to brown.
Yet in the silence, there's beauty found,
In every heart where love is bound.

Gazes reflect on what might have been,
In every fracture, a tale begins.
Through shattered glass, the light breaks free,
In the ruins of tomorrow, we seek to see.

Hope arises amidst fallen grace,
In every loss, a new embrace.
As spirits wander through dust and stone,
Gazing at the ruins, we're never alone.

In the Breath of What Remains

In the quiet dawn, life stirs anew,
Whispers of dreams, a gentle hue.
Each moment a breath, fleeting yet dear,
In the breath of what remains, we find cheer.

Time doesn't pause, it moves with grace,
Carrying echoes of each warm embrace.
In memories woven, the heart expands,
In the breath of what remains, we understand.

The rustle of leaves, a song of the past,
In every heartbeat, shadows are cast.
Yet through the sorrow, we learn to grow,
In the breath of what remains, love's glow.

Turning towards light, away from fear,
Facing the future, eyes crystal clear.
Each step a promise, each day a gain,
In the breath of what remains, we endure the pain.

Through joy and heartache, we create our way,
Finding strength in what words can't say.
Together we stand, in every refrain,
In the breath of what remains, love will remain.

Shades of Light in Evaporating Clouds

In the morning's gentle glow,
Colors dance with soft delight,
Whispers of the day unfold,
In shades of light, the sky takes flight.

Clouds that part, revealing dreams,
Drifting slowly, twilight's grace,
Each hue tells of stories past,
In every curve, a hidden place.

Fleeting moments softly fade,
As shadows stretch and linger long,
The canvas shifts, then gently sways,
In harmony, life's fleeting song.

Dappled rays through branches weave,
Painting scenes of love and time,
Nature's brush reveals the truth,
In every stroke, a verse, a rhyme.

Breathless whispers meet the breeze,
Like secrets shared beneath the sun,
The world transforms, a bright façade,
In shades of light, we become one.

The Lingering Echo of Old Hopes

In quiet corners of the heart,
Memories whisper prayers of light,
A distant gleam, a wistful spark,
The echoes linger, day and night.

Faded visions, dreams once bright,
Haunt the shadows of the mind,
With every sigh, a gentle tug,
Old hopes seek a path to bind.

Through tangled paths of time we roam,
Chasing whispers on the breeze,
A symphony of what was lost,
In softest tones, a heart's unease.

Yet in the twilight's soft embrace,
Resilience blooms, a fragile grace,
For every echo holds the key,
To rise anew, to find our place.

In the stillness, strength can grow,
From ancient seeds, possibilities,
For every echo sings a tune,
Of hope that swells like distant seas.

Constellations in the Ashen Sky

Beneath the cloak of twilight's veil,
A tapestry of stars unfolds,
In ashen hues, the night reveals,
Stories waiting to be told.

Celestial maps of dreams obscure,
Glowing softly in the dark,
Each pinprick light, a guiding star,
Igniting hope, igniting spark.

Through the silence, whispers roam,
Carried on a cosmic breeze,
The constellations, their embrace,
Awakening the soul with ease.

Every flicker tells a tale,
Of love, of loss, of journeys far,
In the ashen sky, we find our way,
Guided by each glowing star.

As night fades and dawn draws near,
The memories drift, yet linger still,
In constellations brightly sewn,
We find the strength to chase our will.

Waking to a World Redefined

In the hush of morning's breath,
Reality begins to shift,
Awakening with every dawn,
A world transformed, a precious gift.

Colors bloom in vibrant hues,
Each moment births a brand new scene,
In the tapestry of life we weave,
A narrative rich and serene.

With open eyes, we start anew,
Reimagining what's come before,
Boundless possibilities arise,
Beyond each threshold, we explore.

Echoes of the past may fade,
Yet lessons linger in our hearts,
In this world redefined, we grow,
Finding strength in fresh new starts.

Emmbracing change, we boldly stride,
With dreams alight, we're not confined,
For in this moment, we ignite,
A life anew, a world refined.

A Soul's Journey Through the Rubble

Amidst the bricks, a whisper calls,
Echoes of feet in the shadowed halls.
Ghosts of laughter linger near,
In every crack, a hidden tear.

A heart once vibrant, now is still,
As memories press with an iron will.
Each step is heavy, burdened by the past,
In ruins of hope, shadows are cast.

The sky above tells tales of light,
In the chasms deep, I seek the bright.
A journey taken, but never alone,
Through rubble and dust, a spirit has grown.

With every stone, a story unfolds,
Of sacrifice made and courage bold.
Through the sorrow, a seed takes root,
From the ashes rises a new pursuit.

As I wander, the dawn begins to break,
A fragile peace in the silence I make.
From the whispers of loss, I now ascend,
A soul's journey, to begin again.

Songs of a Sinking Sun

Across the sky, the colors blend,
A symphony where day must end.
Hues of orange kiss the blue,
A fleeting moment, fading view.

The ocean waves hum a soft tune,
As shadows dance beneath the moon.
With each dip, the daylight sighs,
While stars awaken in velvet skies.

A tranquil heart, yet heavy still,
Yearns for warmth amid the chill.
As the sun sinks low, dreams rise anew,
In whispered tales of love, so true.

Golden rays give way to night,
In darkness, we find hidden light.
Every moment is a fleeting grace,
As time drips slow, leaving its trace.

With the twilight, hopes shall soar,
In the deepening calm, we seek for more.
Songs of a sinking sun will play,
In our hearts, they shall forever stay.

Where Memory Meets the Horizon

At the edge where land meets sea,
Silent echoes call to me.
Each wave that crashes, whispers low,
A dance of ages, ebb and flow.

Moments lost in the fading light,
Drift like dreams into the night.
Carried forth on gentle tides,
Where memory, like water, glides.

The horizon holds my scattered past,
A tapestry woven, shadows cast.
In every dawn, a story reborn,
From the old, the new is worn.

Beneath the sky, I stand alone,
Between what's known and the unknown.
With every breeze, I feel the call,
As where I go, I carry all.

The sun dips low, the stars ignite,
In the embrace of coming night.
Where memory meets the gathering dark,
My spirit sails, leaves its mark.

Beneath the Ruins of Forgotten Joy

Amidst the ashes, whispers sigh,
Echoes linger, asking why.
Faded laughter, shadows dance,
Memories lost in a fleeting glance.

Time once bright, now cloaked in gray,
Beneath the rubble, dreams decay.
Silent cries of hearts once bold,
In the ruins, stories told.

Fragments scatter in the breeze,
Life's sweet promise, brought to knees.
Beneath the surface, hope may still grow,
In the depths of despair, we learn to sow.

Yet in the silence, a spark ignites,
A glimmer of love in the bleakest nights.
Though joy may fade, it leaves a trace,
In hidden corners, we find our place.

So let the wind carry our plight,
Beneath the ruins, we find the light.
With every tear, a seed is sown,
In the garden of souls, we're never alone.

The Poetry of Broken Horizons

In twilight's gleam, the shadows creep,
Promises fade, secrets we keep.
Horizons blur, dreams take flight,
Lost in the ink of fading light.

Beneath the weight of countless sighs,
We weave our tales beneath starry skies.
Each broken line, a story new,
In the depths of darkness, we find the true.

Through shattered glass, we seek the dawn,
Where hope is born, and fears are drawn.
With every fracture, a voice reborn,
In the poetry of pain, we are worn.

Yet in the chaos, beauty remains,
Life's simple truths amidst the pains.
With every stumble, we rise again,
Writing the verses of our own refrain.

So let us dance on broken ground,
In the echoes of dreams, we are found.
With every heartbeat, we carry the weight,
Of the poetry of broken fate.

Time's Embrace of Wounded Souls

In the corners of forgotten schemes,
Time cradles the remnants of shattered dreams.
Wounded souls journey through the haze,
Searching for peace in a world of blaze.

Each tick a reminder of battles fought,
In the embrace of time, we are caught.
Layers of history etched in our skin,
With every heartbeat, a new tale begins.

Together we wander, hand in hand,
In the silence of night, we make our stand.
With every scar, a story to tell,
In the arms of time, we learn to dwell.

Though shadows loom and darkness stirs,
We find our strength in whispered words.
With every sunrise, hope finds its place,
In the embrace of time, we find our grace.

So let the clock tick with patient pride,
Through every tide, we will abide.
For in the wounds, our spirits mend,
In time's embrace, we rise again.

The Spine of Time and Other Ghosts

On the spine of time, ghosts linger near,
Whispers of ages, soft and clear.
Echoes of laughter, shadows of love,
In the still of night, they rise above.

Through the corridors of forgotten years,
We walk with shadows, face our fears.
Every heartbeat a tale untold,
In the canvas of time, our lives unfold.

Yet in the dark, a spark may shine,
Guiding the lost, a brighter line.
The ghosts remind us of paths once crossed,
In the tapestry of time, we find what's lost.

Though specters haunt the edges of day,
They teach us love in their ghostly way.
With every sigh, we breathe them in,
In the spine of time, our journeys begin.

So let the echoes speak their plea,
In the dance of memories, we are free.
For every ghost holds a piece of the past,
In the spine of time, our shadows are cast.

Mirrors of What Once Was

In the glass, reflections fade,
Whispers of the dreams we made.
Shadows dance in silent night,
Fading thoughts, lost from sight.

Time has etched its gentle trace,
Memories weave a tender lace.
Each moment, a fleeting spark,
Illuminates the endless dark.

Once, we laughed beneath the sun,
Now only echoes, memories spun.
Yet in the heart, they softly gleam,
The fragments of a shattered dream.

Like autumn leaves on a stream,
They drift away, a silent theme.
Yet in the stillness, love remains,
Softly spoken, in gentle refrains.

In every crack, a story told,
Of warmth and joy, and hearts of gold.
Mirrors may shatter, truth may bend,
But echoes linger, never end.

Beneath the Echoing Stars

In the night, the heavens sigh,
As whispers twinkle from on high.
Each star holds secrets, old and wise,
Reflecting dreams in shadowed skies.

Beneath the glow, the earth unfolds,
With tales of love and journeys bold.
Night breezes carry hopes anew,
Guiding hearts, both brave and true.

Every constellation shines bright,
Mapping paths of forgotten light.
They speak of destinies in flight,
Underneath the velvet night.

In silence, wishes merge and blend,
A cosmic dance that knows no end.
We cast our dreams into the air,
Trusting fate, as we declare.

With every heartbeat, the stars align,
Filling souls with a spark divine.
Beneath the echoing stars we stand,
Connected by fate's unseen hand.

When Roots Embrace the Stone

In the quiet, roots intertwine,
Grasping earth where shadows shine.
Silent strength in tangled thread,
Holding fast where fears have led.

Through cracks in stone, they push and grow,
Defying odds, embracing flow.
In resilience, life finds its way,
Turning night into bright day.

With every storm, they twist and bend,
Yet their journey does not end.
In steadfast union, they remain,
Through joy and sorrow, loss and gain.

Nature's dance, a timeless tune,
Binding all beneath the moon.
In sacred soil, their whispers blend,
Uniting strife, where paths may bend.

Roots in stone, a tale so wise,
Of strength that blooms while shadows rise.
Together, they defy the odds,
In harmony, beneath the gods.

A Journey Through the Unseen

In twilight's hush, we find our way,
Through secrets held by night and day.
With open hearts and curious minds,
We touch the realms that fate unwinds.

Veils of mystery, softly drawn,
Guide our steps until the dawn.
Each breath a step, each glance a clue,
In shadows deep, we push on through.

The whispers of the past collide,
With wishes cast upon the tide.
Through unseen paths, we bravely roam,
Embracing the unknown as home.

Every heartbeat fuels the quest,
A journey where the soul finds rest.
With every thought, a portal bends,
To worlds unseen, where silence mends.

At journey's close, we stand anew,
With wiser hearts and skies of blue.
For in the unseen, we define,
Our stories lived, our dreams entwined.

The Fragile Beauty of Letting Go

In the hush of twilight's glow,
We release what we used to know.
Like petals drifting from the tree,
Letting go sets the spirit free.

Each memory, a gentle sigh,
A whisper as the moments fly.
In the dance of wind and song,
We find the place where we belong.

With every tear that falls like rain,
We shed the weight of silent pain.
For in the loss, a seed is sown,
A fragile beauty, yet still grown.

The heart, though tender, learns to mend,
Through brokenness, we find our end.
A tapestry of light and shade,
In letting go, new paths are made.

So here we stand, hand in hand tight,
Ready to embrace the night.
With open hearts, we face the dawn,
In fragile beauty, we move on.

A Tapestry of Wounds and Wonders

Threads of pain woven through time,
Each scar a story, each stitch a rhyme.
In the fabric of life, we find our way,
A tapestry of hopes at play.

With every wound, new colors blend,
Healing whispers that refuse to end.
In shadows cast, the light is bold,
A tale of wonders yet untold.

Through valleys deep and mountains high,
The spirit dances, cannot deny.
With every tear, every laugh we borrow,
We weave a future bright with tomorrow.

In the depths of night, we find our song,
A symphony of where we belong.
Each note a reminder, each chord a sign,
In wounds and wonders, our hearts align.

So let us embrace this intricate weave,
In the beauty of with and believe.
For life's true art is in the scars,
A tapestry of dreams and stars.

In the Wake of Dreams Unraveled

As dawn kisses the night goodbye,
We trace the remnants, watch them fly.
In the wake of dreams once bright,
We gather fragments in the light.

With each whispered hope that fades,
We learn to dance in the charades.
Threads of silver against the gray,
In unraveling, we find our way.

What once was whole now softly bends,
Yet in the break, a joy transcends.
For dreams create a tapestry,
Of love and loss, of you and me.

In the echoes of what could be,
We find the courage to be free.
For in the wake, a new dawn spills,
In every heart, a whisper fills.

So here's to all the dreams we chase,
In their wake, we find our place.
Embracing all that life bestows,
In the beauty of dreams, we grow.

Beneath the Weight of Broken Wings

Beneath the weight of broken wings,
A silent song of longing sings.
In the shadows, we learn to soar,
Finding strength in what we bore.

The sky may seem too far away,
Yet hope ignites the light of day.
With every stumble, every fall,
We rise again, we heed the call.

Each feather lost, a lesson learned,
In the ashes, passion burned.
As storms may rage and skies may weep,
We gather courage from the deep.

Through trials faced, the heart expands,
With trembling faith, we make our stands.
In brokenness, a spirit sings,
Resilient souls beneath their wings.

So let us learn to love the scars,
For they shine bright like distant stars.
Beneath the weight, we come alive,
In broken wings, we learn to thrive.

Pieces of a Forgotten Song

Whispers of notes lost in the night,
Echoes of melody take their flight.
Fragments of dreams scattered around,
Ghosts of a symphony, barely found.

Time wears the edges, softens the sound,
Each word a memory, forever bound.
Notes linger gently, a sigh on the breeze,
Fading like shadows beneath the trees.

Singing of moments that once seemed bright,
Harmonies fading into the twilight.
The heart keeps the rhythm, though times have changed,
A ballad of hope that has now been estranged.

Each note a heartbeat, a story untold,
Whispers of feelings that silently fold.
In the quiet, a spark ignites the flame,
Reminding us softly of love's sweet name.

So here in the silence, we gather the parts,
The fragments of visions that fill our hearts.
With a breath, we cherish what has come and gone,
Finding together the pieces of song.

Gathering Clouds of Tomorrow

Veils of gray gather, painting the sky,
Whispers of change as soft winds sigh.
Nature prepares for the coming of rains,
A promise of life where hope remains.

Each droplet an echo of dreams that once flew,
Cleansing the earth, and the heart anew.
Beneath the dark blanket, seeds start to stir,
Awakening warmth where the shadows were.

Colors will burst as the clouds begin weep,
Breaking the silence, a promise to keep.
Life finds a way, through sorrow and strife,
As storms give way to the beauty of life.

In the distance, a glimmer of light,
Guiding the wanderers lost in the night.
As rain dances down, a symphony plays,
Crafting a vision of brighter days.

So gather your hopes like the clouds far above,
Embrace the transformation and share the love.
For each storm that comes, with thunder and might,
Brings forth the dawn, and the warmth of the light.

Beneath the Wreckage

Silent remains where the dreams have decayed,
Memories linger in shadows arrayed.
Among the ruins, whispers of pain,
Life waits for warmth, for healing to reign.

Beneath the rubble, stories reside,
Fragments of laughter and tears have cried.
In corners where light dares not to tread,
Hope finds a way, where the heart has fled.

Beauty emerges from scars left behind,
In each piece of wreckage, a chance to unwind.
Resilience blooms where despair once lay,
Transforming the night into beautiful day.

Listen, the echoes of voices yet pure,
Carrying strength in their soft, silent lure.
From ashes of heartache, new dreams will arise,
Brimming with promise that never truly dies.

So gather the pieces, let love lead the way,
Build from the past, let the heart freely sway.
For even in darkness, the light shall ignite,
Beneath all the wreckage, hope shines so bright.

The Quiet of Renewal

In stillness, the world takes a breath in stride,
Moments of silence, where peace does abide.
Winter's retreat, as spring starts to sing,
A promise of life in the warmth it will bring.

Softly, the flowers break free from their sleep,
All around nature, secrets to keep.
Each petal unfolding, revealing anew,
Colors emerge in a vibrant debut.

The air hums with whispers of skies turning blue,
An orchestra playing, fresh melodies brew.
Butterflies dance in a tapestry spun,
Under the warmth of the glowing sun.

New paths awaken, forgotten dreams clear,
Embracing the change in the atmosphere.
The heart finds its rhythm with each gentle sigh,
In the quiet of renewal, we learn how to fly.

So cherish the stillness, the moments we hold,
In the quiet of spring, where stories unfold.
Each heartbeat a promise, each breath a delight,
In the hush of renewal, all things feel right.

In the Space Between

Between the stars, a whisper glows,
Silent secrets, where no one knows.
In twilight's hush, dreams intertwine,
A tapestry of thoughts divine.

Echoes of laughter, soft and bright,
Mirages linger in the night.
The space between, a gentle wave,
Carries the hopes that we still crave.

Fleeting moments, like grains of sand,
Slipping through an outstretched hand.
Yet in this void, we find our peace,
A stillness where our worries cease.

The universe, a canvas wide,
Colors of time, our hearts abide.
In galaxies that swirl and spin,
We seek the answers deep within.

So cherish dreams that dare to soar,
In the space between, forevermore.
A cosmos beckons with each sigh,
For in our hearts, the stars will lie.

Relics of Hope

Among the ruins, shadows creep,
Stories of old, waiting to speak.
Fragments linger of brighter days,
Whispers of love in faded rays.

Time has woven its secret thread,
In every corner where we tread.
Relics of hope, memories saved,
In hearts where the bravest are braved.

Courage ignites in darkened halls,
Echoes of strength when the silence calls.
From ashes, new dreams arise,
Casting away despair and lies.

Each stone a tale of trials faced,
In the sunlight, a path is traced.
Through cracks and flaws, life will bloom,
In sacred silence, dispelling gloom.

So hold these relics, let them shine,
For from the ruins, our spirits twine.
With every heartbeat, hold them close,
In fragile hope, we find the most.

A New Dawn Over Ruins

As sunbeams crown the silent ground,
A hush descends, peace is found.
In tears of night, the dark withdraws,
Awakening light, nature's laws.

Amidst the rubble, colors flare,
Life reclaims, a vibrant air.
Each dawn, a promise, fresh and pure,
In shadows past, we shall endure.

The past's embrace, a bittersweet guide,
With every step, we turn the tide.
New horizons paint the sky,
Hope reborn as we learn to fly.

Gentle whispers greet the day,
With every breath, we find our way.
Through the wreckage, the spirit cries,
A symphony of sweet goodbyes.

So let the dawn, like fire, reign,
Over the ruins, wash away pain.
In every heartbeat, life finds grace,
A new beginning in time's embrace.

The Heartbeat of Undying Life

In the quiet pulse, life does thrum,
Earth's rhythm echoes, a constant hum.
From mountain peaks to ocean's breath,
In every moment, dance with death.

Through stormy nights and sunny days,
The heartbeat whispers in myriad ways.
Through ancient roots and tender shoots,
Life's saga sings in vibrant loots.

In every tear, a story lies,
In every smile, a sunrise.
The circle spins, an endless flow,
In this embrace, we come to know.

Unity found in the wild dive,
In every heart, the will to thrive.
Life's essence beats, a timeless song,
In undying dreams, we all belong.

So listen close, the pulse is near,
In every heartbeat, shed your fear.
For in this dance, we learn to strive,
In love's embrace, we are alive.

Blossoms in the Ashes

Amidst the fire, new dreams rise,
Petals unfold beneath grey skies.
Life finds a way through scorching plight,
Hope springs forth in tender light.

From blackened earth, a seedling sprouts,
Whispers of joy drown out the doubts.
In every crack, resilience gleams,
Nature's voice speaks of lost dreams.

With every dawn, a brighter hue,
A tapestry of gold and blue.
In every heart, a story grows,
Of beauty found where no one knows.

The ashes cool, but warmth remains,
A dance of life within our veins.
We rise like blossoms, pure and free,
From the shadows, we learn to be.

So let the past, in silence rest,
We carry on, with hope, we're blessed.
Each moment lived, a fragrant sigh,
In ashes, life will never die.

Stitches of the Unseen

In quiet seams, our stories weave,
Silent whispers, hearts believe.
Threads of fate in colors bright,
Bind together wrong and right.

Shadows linger, yet we stand tall,
Held by ties that never fall.
Invisible hands, through joy and tears,
Stitch the fabric of our fears.

From tangled paths, we find our way,
Crafting hope in shades of grey.
Each knot a lesson, softly sewn,
In every heart, the truth is grown.

Though visions fade, our spirits soar,
In every stitch, we ask for more.
Embrace the seams, the unseen light,
Together we can face the night.

And in the quilt of shared embrace,
Love's the thread that holds the space.
With every stitch, we intertwine,
Creating bonds that brightly shine.

Chasing Shadows in Shattered Mirrors

In shards of glass, reflections fray,
Chasing dreams that slip away.
Fragments of light, a fleeting smile,
Echoes linger, lost for awhile.

A dance of shadows in twilight's hue,
Hiding truths we thought we knew.
Through broken frames, our faces blend,
Seeking solace, hearts to mend.

In every crack, a story tells,
Of laughter, love, and silent spells.
Fleeting glimpses of what could be,
Mirrors shatter, yet souls are free.

Unraveled threads of time and space,
We find ourselves in shadows' grace.
Though mirrors break, our spirits shine,
In every piece, a love divine.

So chase the shadows, let them guide,
Through every scar, we learn to bide.
In shattered dreams, we find our way,
Reflections of hope alive each day.

The Essence of Forgotten Whispers

In twilight's hush, where secrets dwell,
Forgotten tales, a silent spell.
Whispers dance on gentle breeze,
Carrying echoes through the trees.

Beneath the stars, old memories fade,
Yet in their warmth, new dreams are made.
A sigh of past, a tender sigh,
In every moment, time slips by.

The essence flows like rivers deep,
In haunting dreams where shadows sleep.
We listen close for ancient lore,
For every heartbeat, there's much more.

With every breath, the whispers call,
To rise again, to stand up tall.
Embrace the moments lost in time,
For in their depths, our souls will climb.

And when the night brings forth its song,
We'll gather strength, where we belong.
In forgotten whispers, we shall find,
The essence of love, forever kind.

Remnants of a Dying Light

Fading whispers in the night,
Ghosts of dreams take their flight.
Stars once bright begin to weep,
As shadows fall, the silence creeps.

Echoes of laughter lost in time,
Memories linger, a quiet rhyme.
The glow that once ignited the skies,
Now flickers low, with weary sighs.

Gentle breezes carry the ache,
Carving paths through hearts that break.
In twilight's grasp, we feel the mend,
Of all that's broken, to the end.

Yet hope endures, though dimmed and slight,
A spark within the dying light.
Resilience fuels the human race,
In every loss, we find our place.

From ashes rise, new flames ignite,
In darkness born, we seek the bright.
A tapestry of love and strife,
Threads of time weave back to life.

Shadows of Tomorrow's Dawn

When night retreats, a whisper calls,
The future waits where darkness falls.
In dreams we chase, through fears we tread,
A path unknown, where courage led.

Fleeting moments of twilight's grace,
Illuminate the shadows' face.
With every step, a story grows,
Of battles fought and paths we chose.

Hopes awaken in morning's glow,
Casting light on seeds we sow.
In shadows deep, potential lies,
The dawn invites, the spirit flies.

We stand on edges, hearts aglow,
Embracing change, we'll learn to flow.
With open arms, we greet the light,
In shadows born, our souls take flight.

Upon the horizon, dreams arise,
In unity, we reach for skies.
The shadows fade, yet wisdom stays,
Guiding us through the winding maze.

When the World Stood Still

In the hush where time draws breath,
A calm descends, a dance with death.
Life held tight in fragile hands,
Moments pause, like shifting sands.

Silent echoes fill the air,
Waves of longing linger there.
Eyes shut tight, we search within,
Finding solace in the thin.

Stillness sings of dreams delayed,
Filling voids where hope has swayed.
Yet in this pause, we learn to feel,
The weight of love, a heart to heal.

When the world stood still, we saw,
Reflections of a greater law.
In gentle whispers, truth unfolds,
As hidden stories start to mold.

So let the stillness shape our way,
Through restless nights and breaking day.
For even in the silent fray,
Life finds rhythm, come what may.

Threads of Ruin and Renewal

Frayed edges in a world once whole,
Tales of sorrow etched in soul.
In ruins laid, foundations shake,
From ashes, hope begins to wake.

Every tear a story spun,
In the darkness, we become one.
With every loss, new strength is drawn,
In silence, hear the coming dawn.

Threads of time intertwine our fates,
Weaving lessons, love creates.
Amidst the wreckage, beauty blooms,
In every heart, a light resumes.

Through cracks of despair, light seeps through,
A tapestry of red and blue.
Resilience stitched with tender hands,
In the fabric of life, we make our stands.

When ruin falls, renewal thrives,
In every ending, a spark survives.
Together we mend what time has burned,
In threads of love, our spirits turned.

When Twilight Meets Dawn

The stars fade softly from the sky,
As whispers of day begin to sigh.
Colors blend in a gentle embrace,
In that sweet moment, time loses pace.

Birds flutter awake from their dreams,
Dew kisses petals, glimmers and gleams.
Shadows retreat, like ghosts from the past,
A promise of light, a spell is cast.

The horizon blushes in shades of gold,
Nature awakens, a story retold.
The world stirs slowly, a breath of new,
In twilight's arms, the dawn breaks through.

Clouds drift lazily, painted in hues,
While trees sway softly, dancing the blues.
Each ray of light a tender caress,
In this perfect moment, we find our rest.

Time holds its breath, a fleeting scene,
When twilight meets dawn, it feels serene.
As day is born, and night slips away,
In the harmony found, forever we stay.

Cinders in the Breeze

The fire has faded, embers glow bright,
Dancing like cinders in the night.
Whispers of warmth, a fleeting refrain,
Echoes of laughter, love's sweet pain.

With every gust, memories fly,
Filled with the dreams we once let die.
Ashes swirl gently, like thoughts in the air,
Fragrant reminders of moments we share.

The canvas of night, a deep velvet hue,
Reflects on the past, on me and you.
Each flicker of flame reveals a scar,
Yet in the darkness, shines a distant star.

Time buries treasures beneath layers of dust,
Yet within our hearts, hope gathers trust.
We gather our cinders, rekindle the spark,
In the embrace of the night, we make our mark.

Fires will fade, but love will ignite,
With cinders in the breeze, we take flight.
Through shadows and storms, we find our way,
Embers of warmth guide us each day.

The Weight of Wounded Wings

Once they soared, in skies so free,
Now they tremble, longing to be.
Feathers tattered, dreams torn apart,
A heavy burden rests on the heart.

Every flap a whisper, every ache a plea,
Carrying the weight of what used to be.
On fragile currents, they struggle to glide,
In search of a haven where they can hide.

Moonlight bathes the scars that they bear,
Silhouettes trembling, caught unaware.
Yet in their plight, a flicker remains,
A hope to rise beyond the chains.

Through the shadows, their spirits will soar,
As they gather strength to face the roar.
For every hardship, a lesson learned,
In the weight of wings, a fire burns.

With courage stitched into every seam,
They rise again, fulfilling their dream.
The journey is painful, the path long and wide,
But with wounded wings, they rise with pride.

In the Wake of Silence

A hush blankets the world tonight,
Each heartbeat echoes, soft and light.
In shadows deep, where whispers cease,
We find our solace, a moment of peace.

The stars above, they softly gleam,
In the wake of silence, we dare to dream.
Thoughts drift gently, like leaves on a stream,
In the stillness, hope begins to beam.

Memories flutter in the quiet air,
Stories untold, waiting to share.
In shared glances, a language profound,
In the wake of silence, love is found.

Time pauses gently, as we unite,
In this sacred stillness, all feels right.
Together we breathe, letting go of the noise,
In the wake of silence, we find our poise.

As dawn approaches, the shadows fade,
Our hearts are lighter, unafraid.
In this precious moment, we come alive,
In the wake of silence, together we thrive.

The Last Echo of Broken Lullabies

Soft whispers dance in shadows deep,
Memories linger where secrets keep.
Once soothing songs now fade to gray,
Lost in the night, they drift away.

Cradled in dreams, they softly sigh,
Echoes of love that slowly die.
A heart once tender, now feels the chill,
Broken lullabies haunt me still.

Beneath the stars, the silence weaves,
A tapestry of what belief leaves.
In corners dark, the shadows play,
Fleeting moments of yesterday.

As dawn approaches, hope's light creeps,
Yet in the stillness, sorrow sleeps.
The last echo fades, a gentle plea,
For times when you were here with me.

Fading into the morning's embrace,
I search for your warmth in empty space.
Though love may wane, the heart still tries,
To hold onto the last lullabies.

Finding Solace in the Fray

Amidst the chaos, I find my ground,
In turbulent waters, peace can be found.
Whispers of comfort sweep through the storm,
A guiding light, so safe and warm.

Fractured paths that twist and turn,
Lead me to places where passions burn.
In the midst of strife, I hear a song,
A melody sweet, where I belong.

Strung like the stars in a velvet night,
Hope glimmers softly, a flickering light.
Through tangled thorns and jagged stone,
I carve my path; I stand alone.

Though battles rage and shadows creep,
A treasure lies in the heart that keeps.
Finding solace in the fray,
I forge my spirit, come what may.

In every heartbeat, I feel the fight,
Resilience born from the darkest night.
With every step, I make my claim,
Finding solace, peace in the flame.

Cerulean Skies, Cracked Foundations

Beneath the vast and cerulean dome,
I wander through dreams, searching for home.
Cracked foundations, the world feels frail,
Yet beauty lingers in every trail.

The sun spills gold on an open field,
Nature's embrace, a heart revealed.
With every breath, I taste the air,
A promise of hope, a whisper of care.

In shadows cast by the fading light,
I chase the echoes of lost delight.
Though cracks may mar the earth below,
The sky remains a canvas aglow.

Through storms that pass and clouds that weep,
I find strength in love that runs deep.
For in the fractures, life will grow,
As cerulean skies continue to flow.

Each broken piece tells tales untold,
Of bravery, warmth, and hearts of gold.
In this imperfect, fragile place,
I find my spirit, my sacred space.

Twilight's Lament

As twilight falls, the world turns gray,
Whispers of night are here to stay.
A soft lament in the fold of dusk,
Fleeting hours, memories husk.

Shadows stretch, embracing the night,
A chorus of crickets, a soft delight.
In the deepening silence, secrets wake,
Promises made, yet hearts still ache.

Stars ignite in the heavens above,
Fragments of dreams and forgotten love.
Each twinkle a story, a wish afloat,
In twilight's arms, we silently gloat.

The moon rises high, a guardian wise,
Bathed in silver, where sorrow lies.
In every heartbeat, a soft refrain,
Twilight whispers our joy and pain.

So let the night cradle what's lost,
In the arms of darkness, we pay the cost.
For in twilight's lament, we find our way,
Between the shadows, we learn to stay.

Unfurling the Shattered Bloom

In shadows deep, a flower bends,
Its fragile petals, once bright, now blend.
Amidst the cracks, new life can rise,
In whispered hopes, the beauty lies.

Each tear that falls becomes a seed,
From brokenness, a heart can bleed.
The sun breaks through, a golden beam,
Awakening the tender dream.

Awake, the bud begins to part,
A dance of colors, nature's art.
Resilience weaves through every stem,
A testament to strength in gem.

With every breath, it reaches wide,
The spirit of the bloom, our guide.
In shattered forms, we find our grace,
Unfurling slowly to embrace.

Beauty thrives in broken spaces,
In silent turns, the heart embraces.
Each bloom unique, a story shared,
Unfurling life, forever bared.

A Journey Beyond the Cracks

Through fissures wide, the light will seep,
A path unfolds where shadows creep.
With every step, a tale is told,
Of strength that grows through cracks of old.

The journey calls, we walk anew,
Embracing every shade and hue.
The scars we bear will fade in time,
A rhythm found, a silent rhyme.

With courage paved on fractured ground,
In chaos, hidden gems are found.
Each journey forged, a map in sight,
To guide us through the endless night.

Beyond the cracks, the dreamers soar,
In whispered winds, they hear the roar.
Each step a dance, each breath a song,
As healing finds where we belong.

Together strong, we travel light,
Through cracks that lead to endless flight.
In every heart, a spark ignites,
A journey bright, our spirits' heights.

The Colors of a Faded Canvas

On canvas worn, the colors blend,
A story lived, each stroke a friend.
In hues of gray, the memories swim,
Where light once danced, now shadows brim.

Yet underneath, the vibrance gleams,
In silent whispers, hold our dreams.
Each layer thick, a life entangled,
In every brush, emotions wrangled.

As colors fade, new shades emerge,
In every sigh, a gentle urge.
To blend the past with future bright,
Creating art from endless night.

Reviving shades, the heart's sweet hue,
In every tear, anew, we grew.
The faded canvas, a tale of grace,
In time's embrace, our colors trace.

A masterpiece of love and scars,
In gentle strokes, we find the stars.
With every layer, we begin anew,
The colors of our journey true.

Songs from the Fragments

In shattered pieces, melodies ring,
From broken hearts, the notes take wing.
A symphony born from the pain,
In gentle whispers, hope will reign.

Each fragment sings a tale so clear,
Of wounds and healing, far and near.
In every crack, there lies a tune,
Awakening under the silver moon.

Harmony flows from depths unknown,
In songs of loss, we find our tone.
Resilience echoes through the night,
Transforming darkness into light.

With every chord, we rise again,
In unison, we break the chain.
Together strong, in unity,
The songs from fragments set us free.

In every heart, the choir swells,
With ancient stories, it compels.
In shattered pieces, beauty sings,
A symphony of life takes wings.

Whispers of the Ground

In the hush of dawn's first light,
The earth tells tales of night,
Roots stretch deep, secrets kept,
In silence, the living wept.

Leaves murmur soft and low,
To the wind, their stories flow,
Each whisper holds a past,
Glimmers of shadows cast.

Old stones bear witness true,
To battles fought, and skies so blue,
Time unfolds in trails of dust,
In the soil, we place our trust.

Footprints fade, yet linger still,
Memories weave through vale and hill,
Nature's heart beats strong and loud,
Within the cradle of the shroud.

Beneath the weight of life unseen,
The ground holds dreams that might have been,
In calm repose, all things abide,
In whispers, the earth confides.

Echoes of Shattered Dreams

In the fragments of the night,
Dreams scatter, lost from sight,
Echoes call from past's embrace,
Longing for a vanished place.

Hope once soared on wings of gold,
Now stories left untold,
In the silence, shadows creep,
Guarding secrets buried deep.

Each sigh carries a distant tune,
A lullaby beneath the moon,
Reminders of what could have been,
In the ghostly spaces in between.

Yet from ruin, sparks can rise,
In the ashes, truth defies,
Healing whispers in the air,
Breaking free from every snare.

So let the echoes softly chime,
In the rhythm of lost time,
For in the heart where sorrow gleams,
New dawn breaks from shattered dreams.

Rebirth from the Ashes

From charred remains, new life will grow,
In the darkness, hope will glow,
Through the flames, the spirit calls,
To rise again, though the darkness falls.

The phoenix sings a fiery song,
In the struggle, we belong,
Every scar, a tale to tell,
In the journey, we will dwell.

Roots will burst through hardened ground,
In resilience, strength is found,
What was lost can be restored,
Through the ashes, dreams are poured.

Springtime blooms in vibrant hues,
Painting skies with hopeful views,
Life returns in wondrous ways,
In rebirth, we find our praise.

So let the fire cleanse the way,
For in the light, we find our stay,
In every ending, a brand new start,
Rebirth whispers to the heart.

Beneath a Crumbling Sky

Underneath a fading dome,
Where clouds sigh and wander home,
The world trembles in its grief,
Searching for a fleeting leaf.

Each crack reveals a story old,
Of hopes not turned to gold,
In the shadows, echoes remain,
Carried on the breath of pain.

Stars flicker like distant dreams,
Lost within the moon's cold beams,
Yet in darkness, the light can spark,
Finding solace in the dark.

Let the storms rage; let them cry,
For beneath the crumbling sky,
Resilience waits; it does not flee,
In every heart, there lies the key.

So gaze above, beyond despair,
For hope blooms in the thinnest air,
Beneath the ruins, life will thrive,
In every struggle, we revive.

Hearts in the Dust of Change

In shadows where the memories dwell,
Hearts beat softly, casting their spell.
Yet time moves, unyielding and vast,
Leaving whispers of the past.

Amidst the rubble, dreams take flight,
In the silence, we seek the light.
Pieces scattered, hopes rearranged,
Finding strength in the dust of change.

The winds of fate whisper and sigh,
Telling stories of love gone by.
In every heart, there's a spark,
Illuminating the eternal dark.

Change carves lines on our weary skin,
But growth begins where we have been.
Tender roots in the soil remain,
Nurturing life from the heart's refrain.

So here we stand, evolving anew,
Embracing the dust, with skies so blue.
In the echoes of every laugh and cry,
The hearts in the dust learn to fly.

Beneath the Surface of Crumbling Grace

In twilight's glow, the silence speaks,
Secrets hidden beneath the creeks.
Crumbling walls, a story untold,
Where dreams once danced in hues of gold.

Soft whispers linger in the air,
Ghosts of laughter, shadows of care.
Beneath the surface, grace still breathes,
Woven tightly in the autumn leaves.

Time wears down the strongest stone,
Yet beauty lingers, ever known.
Through heartache and loss, we find our place,
In the remnants of crumbling grace.

Fragile threads of hope entwined,
In the ruins, love's boundless mind.
Though the structure may begin to fray,
The heart's resilience will find a way.

So here we gather, hand in hand,
In the spaces where we still stand.
Beneath the surface, life will weave,
A tapestry of hope to believe.

In the Stillness of Forgotten Time

In corners deep where shadows grow,
Whispers of ages faintly flow.
Memories linger, soft and light,
In the stillness of fading night.

Each tick of time, a gentle sigh,
Holding moments that drift and fly.
Forgotten tales of love and strife,
Echo softly, breathing life.

Stillness wraps the world in grace,
As we seek our sacred space.
In hushed breaths, the heart's refrain,
Reminds us we are not in vain.

Lost in seconds, we find the key,
Unlocking doors to what could be.
Though time may fade, the essence stays,
In the echoes of unspoken days.

So let us cherish what remains,
In the stillness, wisdom gains.
For in forgotten whispers' chime,
We dance anew in timeless rhyme.

Resonance of the Lost and Found

In twilight's hush, the echoes play,
Resonance guides the lost away.
Through shadows thick, where silence lies,
The heart believes, though hope may die.

Fragments scattered, hearts once whole,
Seeking solace, a hidden goal.
In the ruins, new paths are traced,
Finding strength in the lost and faced.

The whispers call, a gentle nudge,
Through tangled paths, we will not judge.
Each step forward, echoes unfurl,
In the dance of our woven world.

What once was lost, now softly glows,
In the journey, the spirit grows.
Resonance sings from the depths profound,
Binding the threads of the lost and found.

So let us rise, our voices blend,
In the symphony with no end.
In every heartbeat, love abounds,
In the resonance of the lost and found.

Mirrored Reflections of What Was

In still waters, shadows play,
Whispers of a distant day.
Fragments of a life we knew,
Glimmers of a faded view.

Each ripple tells a tale of old,
Secrets in their depths unfold.
Time's passage, a gentle hand,
Carving dreams in shifting sand.

Reflections dance, then fade away,
Tides of memory drift and sway.
We search for meaning in the glass,
What remains, alas, must pass.

Yet echoes linger, soft and light,
In the quiet of the night.
A reminder of love once near,
Fractured hopes we hold so dear.

As dawn breaks on the mirrored seas,
We gather strength from memories.
And though the past may slip and slide,
In our hearts, it will abide.

The Language of Fallen Petals

Petals whisper to the ground,
Silent stories all around.
Faded hues in soft descent,
Words unspoken, life well spent.

Each petal carries time's embrace,
In their soft and gentle grace.
Nature's script in colors bright,
Tell of loss, of love, of light.

Breeze will read what once was said,
In the dance of flowers dead.
Language written, yet unlearned,
In their fall, new paths are turned.

For in the scattered remnants lie,
Seeds of hope that never die.
From the ground we rise anew,
In petals' stories, we renew.

Listen close and you will find,
The meaning left behind.
In every color, every sigh,
A life lived full, a soft goodbye.

Tides of Change

Waves alongside the sandy shore,
Whispers of an unseen roar.
Each tide carries dreams anew,
Shaping lives with every view.

As day breaks, the waters gleam,
Fleeting like a silent dream.
Ebb and flow, the dance of fate,
Guides us through the open gate.

The ocean teaches, ever wise,
In its depths, no truth belies.
With every crest, we learn to bend,
And to embrace the curves, transcend.

Change is constant, never still,
Nature's heart, it beats with will.
From the depths to the sky's range,
We find solace in the change.

Ride the waves, fear not the storm,
For in the chaos, we are warm.
Tides will shift but never break,
In their motion, we awake.

Waters of Grief

In pools of silence, sorrow hides,
A river flows where heartache bides.
Tears fall gently, soft like rain,
Mirroring the hidden pain.

Memories like ripples spread,
Haunting echoes of the dead.
In each wave that crashes down,
Is the weight of love's lost crown.

Through the depths, we learn to swim,
Finding light when hope feels dim.
In the darkest waters, trust,
That even pain can turn to dust.

Each droplet cradles love's embrace,
In sorrow's depths, we find our place.
Time will guide these waters deep,
Through the shadows, we shall leap.

And as the currents shift and sway,
We find our path along the way.
In the waters of our grief,
Rests the seed of sweet relief.

Through the Veil of Withered Hues

Colors fade as seasons change,
In the stillness, life feels strange.
Leaves fall gently to the earth,
Carrying remnants of their birth.

A tapestry of browns and golds,
Nature's story, softly told.
Through the veil, we glimpse the past,
Moments, fleeting, never last.

Yet in the withering, we see,
Beauty lingers endlessly.
In every crack, a world anew,
Through the layers, life breaks through.

Withered hues remind us still,
Life's a journey, bend to will.
Each season holds a sacred space,
In decay, we find our grace.

Through the veil, we learn to weep,
And through those tears, our hearts can leap.
Embrace the change, let colors blend,
From withered hues, new dreams ascend.

The Flavor of Dust and Dreams

In the quiet corners of the night,
Dust dances softly in faded light.
Dreams whisper secrets of long-lost days,
Where shadows linger in a gentle haze.

Memories brush against the skin,
Taste of longing, where we begin.
Each fragment holds a story untold,
In the warmth of twilight, dreams unfold.

The flavor of hope in every breath,
A silent promise that conquers death.
In the cradle of silence, moments sway,
Carried by the winds that dance and play.

Dust of the past, and dreams of the now,
Intertwined whispers, we take a vow.
To cherish each heartbeat and fleeting glance,
In the realm of dust, we find our chance.

Let the night cradle us in its arms,
As we sink deep into its charms.
A taste like honey, sweet on the tongue,
In the flavor of dreams, forever young.

Rising from the Depths

From the shadows where silence reigns,
A spark ignites, breaking the chains.
Beneath the waves of sorrow's embrace,
Hope floats up to find its place.

Resilience stirs like a sleeping tide,
Waves of courage, we cannot hide.
Emerging bright from the depths below,
A spirit reborn in the afterglow.

With every heartbeat, we push ahead,
Old fears fading, the past is shed.
Like a phoenix soaring high and free,
Strength is rising, can't you see?

In the depths we learned how to survive,
Through the darkness, we come alive.
On the surface, the light becomes clear,
Guiding us onward, shedding fear.

So rise we shall, through storm and strife,
In the dance of shadows, we find life.
Rising from depths with hope as our guide,
In the waters of sorrow, we take pride.

Glimmers of Lost Futures

In the twilight of days long gone,
Glimmers of futures flicker on.
Each lost dream holds a silver thread,
Tales of wonder that never bled.

Stars above whisper softly,
Echoes of promises left, so lofty.
Fleeting glimpses like fireflies dance,
Through the night, they weave a romance.

Memories suspended in the air,
Fragments of joy, moments we share.
Beneath the surface of what could be,
Lies a tapestry waiting to see.

In the heart's secret garden, we roam,
Planting seeds of dreams to call home.
Glimmers of futures that may still rise,
In the depths of the soul, love never dies.

So hold on tight to those shining dreams,
In the currents of time, hope redeems.
Glimmers of lost futures brightly gleam,
Guiding us gently like the sweetest dream.

Raven's Call in Stillness

In the quiet woods, a raven cries,
Echoes through branches, beneath dark skies.
A call that weaves through the misty air,
Awakens the silence, a moment rare.

With wings of shadows, it glides through trees,
Carrying whispers on the evening breeze.
A guardian of secrets, wise and old,
In its presence, we find stories told.

Stillness wraps around like a gentle shawl,
In the heart's chamber, we hear the call.
Embrace the silence, where magic lies,
In the raven's shadow, our spirit flies.

Wisdom threading through the darkened night,
Guiding lost souls back to the light.
In the stillness, we gather our dreams,
Awakening echoes in whispered themes.

Raven's call, a timeless refrain,
In the dance of silence, we feel no pain.
Bound by the night and its gentle thrall,
We find our strength in the raven's call.

When Dreams Collapse into Dust

Winds whisper through shattered glass,
Echoes of laughter lost in time.
Faded hopes upon the grass,
Once they soared, now they climb.

Shadows stretch beneath the moon,
As silent prayers drift away.
Embers blink, a muted tune,
Fading dreams in disarray.

Stars blink out, one by one,
As dawn breaks the night apart.
What was bright is now undone,
Leaving scars upon the heart.

A world once painted in gold,
Turns to ash upon the ground.
Stories etched but never told,
In dust, only ghosts are found.

Yet from ruins, new seeds grow,
Whispers of hope begin to creep.
In each crack, there's life bestowed,
Awakening dreams from sleep.

Revisiting Lost Landscapes

Through the fog, forgotten paths,
Once vibrant colors fade to grey.
Tracing steps my heart now quaffs,
In fields where laughter used to play.

Ruins stand, silent and still,
Memories whisper in the breeze.
Echoes linger, time does thrill,
In every rustle of the trees.

Mountains loom, proud and tall,
While rivers weave their soft embrace.
Nature sings a siren's call,
To all who wander, lost in space.

The skyline painted by sunset,
Touched by hues of deep despair.
A canvas where dreams were met,
Now hangs heavy in the air.

Yet beauty dwells in decay,
In every crack a story breathes.
Revisiting lost landscapes,
Rekindling hope, as time weaves.

The Echo of Faded Footsteps

Footprints wash away in sand,
The tide rolls in, a gentle thief.
Every step, a fleeting brand,
Yet the heart holds on to grief.

Paths once walked are now behind,
Shadows linger where we used to roam.
Memories like whispers bind,
Carving stone, we can't call home.

Silence reigns where we once laughed,
In the stillness, echoes play.
A bittersweet, unbroken craft,
Of moments lost, now tucked away.

As twilight fades into the night,
Stars awaken, ghosts take flight.
Each echo fades beyond our sight,
Leaving only the softest light.

Yet in the dark, a flame will glow,
The journey forged, forever near.
In every echo, love will grow,
Resonating year by year.

Rising from the Relics

From dusty shelves, old stories wake,
Unearthed treasures whisper soft.
Time's embrace, a gentle shake,
From the depths, our dreams aloft.

Forgotten toys and faded cards,
Speak of laughter, joy, and play.
In the silence, no more guards,
As lost spirits find their way.

Relics tell of days gone by,
Held within their weathered grip.
As memories float and sigh,
Every moment, a fleeting trip.

Yet through the wreckage, new paths bloom,
Resilience found in broken seams.
From relics borne, we face our doom,
And rise again to chase our dreams.

The power lies in what was lost,
For in the echoes, voices gleam.
Rising up, at any cost,
We weave anew, we live our dream.

Resurgence in Radiance

In shadows deep, a light breaks free,
Embers glow of what will be.
Hope rekindles, softly glows,
A heart reborn, as spirit flows.

With each dawn, the world awakes,
A melody that softly stakes.
Through tear-streaked paths, we rise anew,
The skies regain their vibrant hue.

In whispers warm, the dreams unite,
As stars above relight the night.
Together we, with courage strong,
Create a world where we belong.

With every storm, the heart takes wing,
Through trials faced, our voices sing.
In radiant hues, our futures spun,
A tapestry of battles won.

So here we stand, hand in hand,
The light of hope, a steady strand.
In resonance, we find our place,
A resurgence built on love and grace.

Remnants of a Broken World

In silent streets, whispers remain,
Echoes captured in the rain.
Shattered dreams in crumbled stone,
A tale of hearts that mourn alone.

Beneath the dust, memories lie,
With every tear, a haunting sigh.
Lost in shadows, yet we seek,
The glimmers of hope, though they feel weak.

In every scar, a story told,
Of battles fought and spirits bold.
Among the ruins, roots take hold,
A sign of life through remnants old.

Yet amidst the chaos, seeds are sown,
With tender care, love brightly grown.
From ashes rise, the phoenix true,
Rebirth found in shades of blue.

So let us weave from threads of pain,
A dream restored, a heart's refrain.
In shattered worlds, we'll find a way,
To build anew with each new day.

The Colors of Remembrance

In hues of time, the past remains,
Each color bright, each tremor gained.
Through vibrant strokes, we paint anew,
The canvas vast, of me and you.

In shades of laughter, tears once shed,
The stories shared, the words unsaid.
From golden days to twilight's grace,
Every moment finds its place.

With every brush, the heart does sing,
Of love and loss, of everything.
The palette swirls with life's embrace,
Colors unite in tender space.

From deep maroons to soothing blues,
In twin reflections, all we choose.
To carry forth the echoes true,
A legacy of me and you.

So let the colors blend and sway,
As memories dance in bright array.
In light of love, we'll find the way,
To honor life, come what may.

A Tattered Canvas of Tomorrow

With frayed edges, dreams unfold,
A canvas worn yet brave and bold.
In each brushstroke, hope is spun,
   A tapestry of all we've done.

In vibrant threads of day and night,
We weave the dark to find the light.
Amidst the fray, our visions soar,
A dance of futures, evermore.

Though storms may tear, and colors run,
Resilience glows in everyone.
In every tear, a chance to mend,
For art of life will never end.

We'll paint the stars across the sky,
And dream of worlds where hearts can fly.
In every hue, a story shared,
A journey lived, a heart laid bare.

So as we stand on paths unknown,
With every step, our seeds are sown.
Through tattered dreams, the morrow gleams,
In unity, we'll chase our dreams.

Ghosts of What Might Have Been

In shadows whisper dreams so pale,
Fleeting thoughts on a forgotten trail.
Echoes linger where hopes once bloomed,
In the silence, regrets are entombed.

Paths not taken, paths unseen,
Futures woven in hopes between.
In every choice, a life anew,
Yet still we ponder what could ensue.

In starlit nights, their faces fade,
Memories linger in dreams we made.
Haunting visions, lost in the mist,
A tender touch of a fleeting kiss.

They dance on the edges of our mind,
Reminders of love we left behind.
A whisper of laughter, a sigh of pain,
Ghosts of what might have been remain.

With every heartbeat, shadows creep,
Awakening sorrows buried deep.
Yet in their presence, we find the light,
Guiding us gently through the night.

The Weight of a Thousand Tomorrows

Beneath the stars, we carry dreams,
The weight of futures torn at the seams.
Every wish a stone in the heart,
Each promise echoes, a solemn art.

With every dawn, the burden grows,
A silent struggle no one knows.
Yet in the shadows, hope does gleam,
A fragile flicker in the unseen.

Time dances forward, yet pulls us back,
Navigating through a veiled track.
In the hourglass, grains of despair,
Anchor our spirits in endless air.

But in the twilight, we'll find our place,
The weight will lessen, we'll feel its grace.
For every tomorrow that's yet to start,
We carry the fire within our heart.

So let us rise with the morning light,
Gather the dreams, let them take flight.
With each step forward, we shall be free,
The weight of tomorrow unburdened, you see.

Dancing on the Edge of Yesterday

In whispers soft, the past will sway,
We find our rhythm in disarray.
With every step, we bridge the gap,
Between the now and memories' map.

Time spins gently, a waltz so fine,
We dance on edges, in realms divine.
In laughter, in tears, we twirl and spin,
Reliving moments, let the dance begin.

Each heartbeat echoes with tales untold,
Of innocence cherished, and dreams of bold.
In familiar faces, shadows play,
Lost in the music of yesterday.

As twilight fades, the music swells,
We follow the echoes where memory dwells.
With fragile steps on the edge we tread,
Dancing on whispers of things unsaid.

Yet as the night draws to its close,
We hold the light of the past that glows.
Embraced by the moments, we'll learn to see,
The dance of yesterday, a part of me.

The Silence that Follows

In the stillness, echoes fade,
Whispers linger in twilight's shade.
Words unspoken, heavy in the air,
The silence follows, a weight to bear.

After the storm, the calm descends,
A space where thought and feeling blend.
In every pause, a heart beats slow,
Life's melody softened, a gentle flow.

Haunting echoes of laughter lost,
In moments cherished, pay the cost.
But in the quiet, a strength we find,
A solace woven, gentle and kind.

In shadows cast by fading light,
We learn to mend the edges tight.
For in the hush, there's also grace,
The silence follows, a warm embrace.

Through every heartbeat, stillness sings,
Of past and present, and all that brings.
In every silence, a chance to grow,
The beauty of peace, in quiet, we know.

The Haunting of Unfinished Stories

In shadows where lost tales abide,
Whispers linger, secrets collide.
Pages torn, ink left to dry,
Ghosts of words, they softly sigh.

Underneath the moon's cold stare,
Fragments of dreams float in the air.
Each chapter calls, each line a plea,
For voices past, to set them free.

The echoes of laughter, past and gone,
Thread through time, a melancholic song.
In the silence, characters roam,
Searching for their narrative home.

Yet still they wait, in dusky light,
For hands to pen their story right.
From the depths, they rise once more,
To weave a tapestry rich and pure.

So listen close, dear heart, beware,
For unfinished tales float everywhere.
Let not their whispers fade away,
Bring them life, give them their say.

Gathering the Pieces of a Clouded Dream

In the haze of twilight's glow,
Fragments sparkle, soft and slow.
A tapestry of thoughts unwind,
Lost in whispers of the mind.

Petals drift upon a stream,
Carried softly, like a dream.
Seek the colors, curve and glide,
Holding truths that seek to hide.

Through the mist, we chase our fate,
Piecing visions; it's not too late.
Breath by breath, they come alive,
In the chaos, we will thrive.

With open hearts, we gather near,
Embracing joys, facing fear.
Shards of hope in every seam,
Stitch our lives, one thread, one dream.

So let us dance in twilight's hue,
Gather the pieces, me and you.
For within each gentle sigh,
Lives a dream that will not die.

The Gentle Art of Picking Up

When shards of silence fill the room,
And shadows stretch, seeking gloom.
With careful hands, we must retrieve,
The beauty in what we believe.

Fallen hopes, like scattered seeds,
Can bloom again, when nurtured needs.
A tender touch, a patient heart,
Can mend what feels like worlds apart.

With every sigh and every tear,
We stitch the moments held so dear.
In quiet strength, we find our way,
Through stormy nights and brighter days.

So gather close those fragile dreams,
In golden light, they softly gleam.
The gentle art of picking up,
Is finding joy within the cup.

With open hands, we join the dance,
Embracing life's uncertain chance.
For every piece, both lost and found,
Leads to love, where hope abounds.

Flickers of Hope in Transience

In moments brief, like sparks of light,
Hope flickers soft in the dead of night.
A flash of beauty, all too rare,
In fleeting time, we learn to care.

Like fireflies that gently gleam,
They guide our hearts with whispered dreams.
Though life may change like shifting sand,
We reach for those flickers, hand in hand.

The petals fall, the seasons sway,
Yet in our hearts, they choose to stay.
For every end brings forth a start,
In the dance of life, we play our part.

So cherish each tender embrace,
In every loss, we find our grace.
For in the brief, we learn to see,
The depth of love, eternally.

Through transience, our spirits soar,
Carrying hopes forevermore.
In every flicker, we find the key,
To live, to love, to truly be.

A Symphony of Fractured Stars

In the vastness, whispers breathe,
Fragments weave a tale of grief.
Echoes dance on broken beams,
Melodies of lost dreams gleam.

Celestial notes in twilight glow,
Each star sings of woes we know.
Harmony in shards remains,
A chorus formed of silent pains.

Across the night, they shimmer bright,
Guiding souls through endless light.
In unity, they find their place,
A symphony of time and space.

Through the darkness, the fragments flare,
A blend of hope and deep despair.
Fractured light, yet still they shine,
A testament to the divine.

With every beat, the cosmos sighs,
A reminder underneath the skies.
For amidst the cracks, new worlds start,
A symphony of fractured heart.

From Pe ashes to Petals

In the silence of the dawn,
Life emerges, reborn and drawn.
From the remnants of despair,
Beauty blossoms, clean and rare.

Once charred by flames of fear and doubt,
Now blossoms where hope pours out.
Petals soft, like whispers kind,
A story of the soul unconfined.

Each layer sheds, a piece renews,
The fragrance speaks of vibrant hues.
Resilience blooms in gentle shrouds,
A dance among the hopeful crowds.

In gardens where the ashes lie,
Life finds ways to touch the sky.
From darkness, light begins to swell,
In every petal, a new tale to tell.

With every breeze, the flowers sway,
A promise of a brighter day.
From the past, we rise and grow,
From ashes deep, new life will show.

Starlight Drifting on the Wind

Whispers carried by the night,
Starlight glimmers, pure and bright.
In the hush, dreams intertwine,
A celestial dance, so divine.

Each sparkle tells a tale untold,
Of ancient realms and treasures bold.
Silhouettes against the dark,
The cosmos hums a gentle spark.

Through the branches, soft and low,
A melody of light and glow.
Drifting whispers, secrets flow,
In the night, they gently grow.

Carried forth on evening's breath,
Life and starlight conquer death.
In the quiet, shadows blend,
As hopes and dreams begin to mend.

With the wind, the starlight flies,
Painting wishes in the skies.
In every breeze, magic sways,
Starlight guiding all our ways.

The Quiet Strength of Scarred Hearts

In the valleys of silent tears,
Lie the echoes of our fears.
Beneath the scars, the heartbeats pound,
Strength resides in hollow ground.

Each mark a tale of battles fought,
Lessons learned, and battles sought.
In quiet strength, we rise anew,
A tapestry of pain and view.

With every wound, resilience breathes,
A spirit woven, never sheathes.
In shadows cast by doubt and strife,
We forge our wounds into new life.

The scars may show a troubled past,
Yet, in their depths, we hold steadfast.
A quiet strength that binds us tight,
Emerging bold, embracing light.

Though the road may twist and bend,
Our scarred hearts learn to transcend.
In the stillness, beauty starts,
The quiet strength of scarred hearts.

Milton Keynes UK
Ingram Content Group UK Ltd.
UKHW020041271124
451585UK00012B/983